200-YEAR-OLD BOWHEAD WHALES!

By Leonard Atlantic

Gareth Stevens
PUBLISHING

Please visit our website, www.garethstevens.com. For a free color catalog of all our high-quality books, call toll free 1-800-542-2595 or fax 1-877-542-2596.

Library of Congress Cataloging-in-Publication Data

Names: Atlantic, Leonard, author.
Title: 200-year-old Bowhead whales! / Leonard Atlantic.
Other titles: Two hundred-year-old Bowhead whales
Description: New York : Gareth Stevens Publishing, [2017] | Series: World's longest-living animals | Includes bibliographical references and index.
Identifiers: LCCN 2016027724| ISBN 9781482456318 (pbk. book) | ISBN 9781482456332 (6 pack) | ISBN 9781482456356 (library bound book)
Subjects: LCSH: Bowhead whale–Juvenile literature. | Longevity–Juvenile literature.
Classification: LCC QL737.C423 A85 2017 | DDC 599.5/276–dc23
LC record available at https://lccn.loc.gov/2016027724

Published in 2017 by
Gareth Stevens Publishing
111 East 14th Street, Suite 349
New York, NY 10003

Designer: Andrea Davison-Bartolotta and Bethany Perl
Editor: Ryan Nagelhout

Photo credits: Cover, pp. 1, 17, 21 Paul Nicklen/National Geographic/Getty Images; pp. 2–24 (background) Dmitrieva Olga/Shutterstock.com; p. 5 Bering Land Bridge National Preserve/Wikipedia.org; p. 7 Encyclopedia Britannica/Universal Images Group/Getty Images; p. 9 (bowhead whale illustration) Suchkova Anna/Shutterstock.com; p. 9 (whale skeleton illustration) Spoiled_Milk/Shutterstock.com; pp. 11,13 Steven Kazlowski/Science Faction/Getty Images; p. 15 (whale fishing illustration) Ken Welsh/Perspectives/Getty Images; p. 15 (harpoons) Alexandru Nika/Shutterstock.com; p. 19 Bobby Haas/National Geographic/Getty Images.

CPSIA compliance information: Batch #CW17GS: For further information contact Gareth Stevens, New York, New York at 1-800-542-2595.

CONTENTS

Boldface words appear in the glossary.

Big and Old

Bowhead whales are some of the longest-living animals on Earth. They are also some of the largest. These gigantic animals live in very cold Arctic waters near the North Pole. They can live for more than 100 years!

Long Bodies

Bowhead whales are sometimes called Greenland whales or Greenland right whales. Most bowhead whales are 50 to 60 feet (15 to 18 m) long. The longest ever found was 65 feet (19.8 m) long!

7

Big Heads

About one-third of a bowhead whale's body is its head. It has a large skull and a big lower jaw. The size of its head makes its body look short and fat! Its thick **layer** of **blubber** keeps its body warm in the cold Arctic waters.

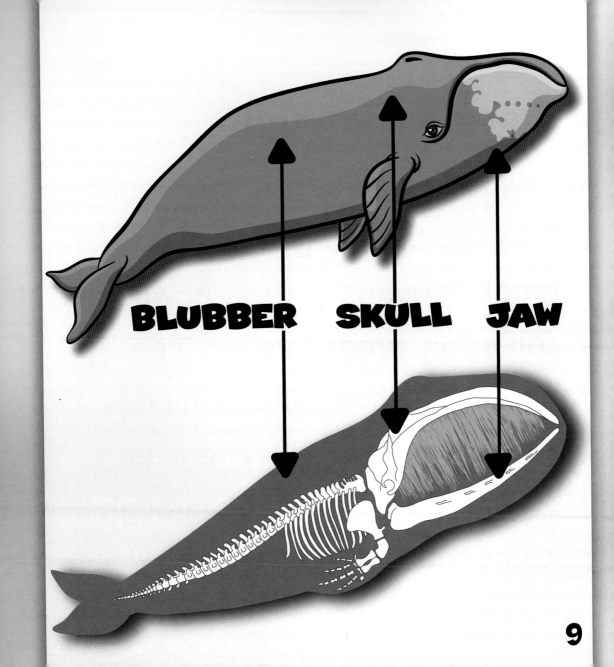

BLUBBER   **SKULL**   **JAW**

9

Breaking Through

Bowhead whales are very strong. They use their large head to break through thick ice. Bowheads can easily break through ice almost 8 inches (20 cm) thick. Some hunters say they've seen bowhead whales break through ice nearly 2 feet (60 cm) thick!

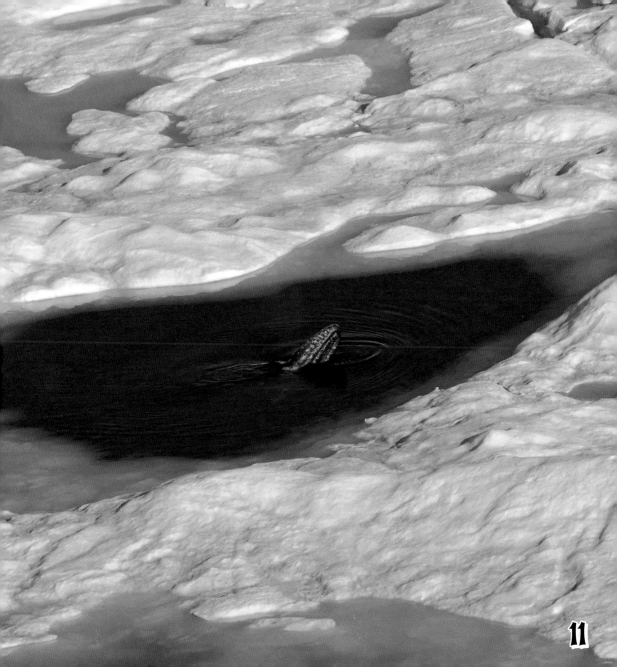

11

Filter Feeders

Bowhead whales don't have teeth. Instead, they have **baleen** that's used to **filter** water the whale takes in. The baleen traps tiny animals called zooplankton, which bowhead whales like to eat. Bowheads have very long baleen—sometimes more than 13 feet (4 m) long!

BALEEN

13

Just How Old?

Teeth are often used to judge an animal's age, but bowhead whales have no teeth. So scientists studied their eyes. Scientists also found stone **harpoon** tips in some bowhead whales. Harpoons haven't been used in over 100 years. Scientists now think bowheads can live over 100 years.

HARPOONS

200 Years?

A huge whale 100 years old is pretty amazing, but scientists discovered something even more amazing. They believe one whale they studied was over 200 years old! That means the whale was likely alive when the White House was built and when Thomas Jefferson became president!

Family Life

Bowhead whales usually live alone or in small groups of 2 or 3. They form larger groups when they migrate, or move over longer **distances**. Groups of up to 14 whales move in a V-shape through the water.

19

Keeping Them Safe

Today, bowhead whales are **endangered** in some places. They have low numbers due to overhunting. They've been harmed by changes in their ocean **habitats** as Earth warms and Arctic ice melts. Scientists are working to **protect** these amazingly old animals from dying out.

GLOSSARY

baleen: plates of long, hard matter hanging in the mouth of some whales and used to gather food

blubber: a layer of fat whales use for warmth

distance: the amount of space between two points

endangered: in danger of dying out

filter: to collect bits from a liquid passing through

habitat: the natural place where an animal lives

harpoon: a spear used in hunting large fish or whales

layer: one thickness of something lying over or under another

protect: to keep safe

FOR MORE INFORMATION

BOOKS

Miller, Sara Swan. *Whales of the Arctic*. New York, NY: PowerKids Press, 2009.

Petrie, Kristin. *Bowhead Whales*. Edina, MN: ABDO Publishing, 2006.

WEBSITES

BBC—Bowhead Whale
bbc.co.uk/nature/life/Bowhead_whale
Find out more about how bowhead whales live long lives on this BBC site.

Bowhead Whale
www.panda.org/what_we_do/endangered_species/cetaceans/about/right_whales/bowhead_whale/
Find out more about how bowhead whales are protected as endangered species.

Bowhead Whales
www.afsc.noaa.gov/nmml/education/cetaceans/bowhead.php
Learn more fun facts about bowhead whales and their long lives here.

INDEX